# DRY STREAK

# DRY STREAK

Leeann Minogue

Dry Streak
first published 2006 by
Scirocco Drama
An imprint of J. Gordon Shillingford Publishing Inc.

4th Printing, 2016

Scirocco Drama Editor: Glenda MacFarlane
Cover design by Terry Gallagher/Doowah Design Inc.
Author photo by Bob Orsted
Printed and bound in Canada

We acknowledge the financial support of the Manitoba Arts Council, The Canada Council for the Arts and the Government of Canada through the Book Publishing Industry Development Program (BPIDP) for our publishing program.


Production inquiries should be addressed to:
Leeann Minogue
Box 56
Griffin, SK S0C 1G0

Library and Archives Canada Cataloguing in Publication

Minogue, Leeann, 1970-
Dry streak/Leeann Minogue.

A play.
ISBN 1-897289-08-1

I. Title.

PS8626.I56D79 2006 C811'.6 C2006-902820-6

J. Gordon Shillingford Publishing
P.O. Box 86, RPO Corydon Avenue, Winnipeg, MB Canada R3M 3S3

# Acknowledgements

It takes a lot of people to fully develop a play. I have many people to thank. My friends at St. Cere were the first writers to hear of this idea—they encouraged me to start writing this story. My long-time friends from the Rosher Invitational camping trip read the very first draft of *Dry Streak* aloud on the beach next to our canoes on a hot summer afternoon and came up with all kinds of helpful advice. The actors in my hometown of Lacadena took a chance on an earlier version of this play (titled *Give 'Er Snoose)* and bravely staged it for their annual dinner theatre, giving me a chance to see these characters come to life for the first time.

The Saskatchewan Playwrights Centre is an invaluable resource for Saskatchewan playwrights. Without the diligent help of dramaturge Ben Henderson, workshops with terrific actors, and the 2004 SPC Spring Festival of New Plays, *Dry Streak* would never have made it to the professional stage. The actors at the Spring Festival and director Bob Metcalfe provided a ridiculous amount of helpful advice and insight. Director Stephen Heatley took an interest in *Dry Streak* at the Spring Festival and has helped to move it forward and put it on its feet.

Saskatchewan has a very strong community of writers, many of whom have been supportive and helpful to a new face in the crowd. I am lucky to be part of a great Regina writing group, the Bees, who have celebrated my successes and failures with equal grace and style.

I am pleased that so many of my family and friends have travelled great distances over icy Saskatchewan roads to see this play. I am especially thankful for my parents, who have sat through many productions, and who have been my most enthusiastic fans all along. And, of course, I am most grateful for my husband Brad, who helped me find time and space to write this play, and who continues to support me in everything I do.

# Time and Setting

This play takes place in Stony Valley, a fictional rural Saskatchewan community in the summer of 1988. In most parts of Saskatchewan's grain growing area this was the second year of extreme drought—a very difficult year for many farmers and for Saskatchewan's farm economy.

None of the locations used in this play require extensive stage settings. Settings can be minimal, using a few key pieces to establish place, for example, a plaid tablecloth over a simple table to indicate a dining room, or a table with a red terrycloth tablecloth with empty beer bottles and an ashtray to indicate a small town bar.

# A Note About the Language

Although the language in this play is not intended to be offensive or crude, some casts or directors may take exception to some of the words that are included in the text. Where necessary, other words or expressions that would maintain the characters' intentions may be substituted.

The "/" slash is used through the text to indicate where the next character interrupts and begins to speak.

# Characters

The Richards Family

| | |
|---|---|
| Olive Richards: | A farm wife in her late 50s or early 60s. Olive is dedicated to her family and community. Dresses in non-descript casual-wear (pants, T-shirts). |
| Peter Richards: | Olive's husband. Peter is a gruff but well meaning farmer in his late 50s, early 60s. Dresses in blue jeans, work shirts, workboots, and agricultural caps. |
| John Richards: | (28) Dresses in jeans, T-shirts, running shoes, and ball caps. |
| Denise (Richards) Smith: | (26) John's sister, Olive and Peter's middle child. She is married with two children and her clothing is stylish, but practical. |
| Charlie Richards: | (24) Peter and Olive's youngest child. Lives in Saskatoon and works at a radio station. Dresses in popular eighties style (red leather jackets, skinny ties, etc). |

Others

| | |
|---|---|
| Kate Allen: | (25) John's new girlfriend. She dresses in 80s punk and alternative fashions and prefers alternative music. |
| Rob Armstrong: | Stony Valley's mayor, newspaper owner / editor, and entrepreneur. He is a friend of Peter, Peter's age. He dresses in khaki pants and shirts. |

## Production History

*Dry Streak* premiered at Persephone Theatre in Saskatoon, Saskatchewan in January, 2006 with the following cast:

PETER Richards ........................................................ Mo Bock
OLIVE Richards .................................................. Lorna Wilson
JOHN Richards .................................................. Skye Brandon
KATE Allen .................................................... Trenna Keating
DENISE Smith .......................................... Jamie Lee Shebelski
CHARLIE Richards ...................................... Rob van Meenan
ROB Armstrong ............................................. Kelly Handerek

Directed by Stephen Heatley
Set Design by Ralph Blankenagel
Costume Design by Theresa Germain
Lighting Design by Mark von Eschen
Stage Manager: Laura Kennedy

# Leeann Minogue

Leeann Minogue grew up in rural Saskatchewan and eventually made the decision to stay. Now she lives on a grain farm in south-eastern Saskatchewan, five miles south of Griffin, with her husband, Brad Barlow, their dog Angus, and two identical cats. *Dry Streak* is her first full-length play. When Leeann is not writing plays and short stories she spends her time playing the piano and teaching lessons, reading, knitting, welding, attempting to avoid housework, and helping out on the farm.

# Act One

## Scene 1

*The dining room of PETER and OLIVE's farmhouse. The stage is set with a table and four chairs. Actors will use the left exit to go to the kitchen; the right exit leads outside.*

*There is a copy of the* Western Producer[1] *on the table.*

*OLIVE is cleaning busily (dusting, or vacuuming). PETER enters from the right, wearing dirty work clothes. He bends down to take off his work boots.*

OLIVE: Oh are you in for coffee already?

PETER: Looks like it.

*OLIVE sets down her cleaning equipment and runs to the kitchen while PETER sits at the table to read the paper.*

*She returns quickly with two empty cups and a coffee pot, and pours coffee for both of them.*

OLIVE: Good timing! I just took some muffins out of the oven.

*She takes the coffee pot back to the kitchen.*

PETER: *(Reading from his paper.)* Listen to this, Olive. The *Western Producer* says it only costs Monsanto six bucks a litre to make Roundup. I gotta pay eighteen bucks for a litre of the stuff. Damn Monsanto. Somebody oughta sue that outfit.

Hmmmmph. Way things are going these days, nobody's gonna be able to afford to farm. Why would they want to? Have to send my own son to the city to work for the winter.

OLIVE: *(Entering, with a plate of muffins and setting them on the table.)* Here. Have one of these. Maybe it'll put you in a better mood.

PETER: I'm not in a bad mood, Olive. Geez. Women. *(He takes a bite of a muffin and chews it with a confused look while he continues to read the paper.)* Olive! What the hell kind of muffin is this?

OLIVE: Carrot. Aren't they moist? I found the recipe in a new book I bought in the city last week.

PETER: *(Shaking his head and setting the muffin down.)* Vegetables in a muffin. What's all this about?

OLIVE: Nothing.

PETER: Don't you have any cinnamon buns? Chocolate cake?

OLIVE: I'm just trying something new, for once. I should've known better, after living with you all these years. I'll get you a cinnamon bun.

*OLIVE exits to the left and returns quickly with a cinnamon bun on a plate. She sets it on the table in front of PETER, who looks at her expectantly.*

PETER: Butter?

OLIVE: Oh alright.

*She goes back to the kitchen and comes back with a butter dish and knife.*

PETER: I know what you're doing. I know exactly what

you're doing. You're trying to impress this girl that's coming out from Calgary with John today.

OLIVE: Well, Kate sounds like such a *nice* girl. And she's from such a good family.

PETER: Like we're not a good family.

OLIVE: Peter! Her father's a diplomat!

PETER: Nothing wrong with farming Olive.

OLIVE: Oh, I know, but Kate's life just sounds so exciting. Travelling all over the world. Meeting so many people.

PETER: Oh boy. This is really going to be something, isn't it? My son. Dating a *vegetarian.*

OLIVE: Oh Peter, quit worrying about that. A lot of young people in the city are vegetarians these days.

PETER: Well not out here they aren't. Geez Olive. Just because she doesn't eat meat doesn't mean you have to start hiding vegetables in everything.

OLIVE: I just wanted to try something new, Peter.

PETER: Geez Olive. Show a little sense, will ya? If John's new girl doesn't like us as we are, she can get the first bus out. City girl.

OLIVE: John is twenty-eight years old. We knew this day would come. And he sounded *so* excited about her over the phone this winter.

PETER: Hmmmmph. She sounds like some kinda flake. Moving around from place to place all her life.

OLIVE: Peter Richards. You will be nice to this girl. She's only staying for three days. And we want this to work out for John.

PETER: Hmmmmph. She'll take one look at the place and head straight back to the city.

OLIVE: Peter!

PETER: A fancy-living high-flying *vegetarian*. Imagine. Working as a *ski instructor*. And what was John doing? Shelling out good money for skiing lessons. Gravity would've got him to the bottom sooner or later.

OLIVE: Most of the kids that try skiing take a lesson.

PETER: And why the hell was he *skiing* in the first place? We sent him to Calgary to work. Save some money. Not spend a fortune *skiing*.

OLIVE: Now Peter, John works hard. It's good for him to have a little fun once in a while.

PETER: Yeah, yeah. He works hard. But geez. Couldn't he just find someone from here? He doesn't need to go bringing home some *city* woman that won't understand how things are out here.

OLIVE: You know there aren't many girls his age out here.

PETER: Hmmmph. Nothing wrong with that James girl.

OLIVE: Sheila's engaged. She's marrying the new Wheat Pool agent.

PETER: Hmmmph.

OLIVE: Peter. I'm sure if John likes Kate, we'll like her. And she's not spoiled or lazy. She had a job all winter.

PETER: Depends on what you call a 'job'. *(Looking back to his paper.)* Government's giving out spring seeding loans. Twenty-five bucks an acre, and only nine and a half percent interest.

OLIVE: *(On her way to the kitchen.)* Oh—that's a much better rate than last year. I can feel it—1988's going to be a great year.

PETER: Not if it doesn't rain. Christ. I'll be seeding into a dustbowl. Don't know how anything's gonna grow out there.

OLIVE: *(From the kitchen.)* I *thought* I heard something! Peter! John's here! He's driving down the lane! He's early!

PETER: You don't have to shout about it.

OLIVE: You haven't seen him for almost seven months. Aren't you excited?

PETER: He's been in Calgary, Olive, not up in the damn space shuttle.

OLIVE: I thought I'd have another few hours! Do you think I should change my clothes? How's my hair?

PETER: What? Olive, she's a *vegetarian*, for Christ's sake. It's not the Pope coming to stay.

OLIVE: I just want us to make a good impression.

PETER: Impression?

OLIVE: I hope it's not too cold in the guest room. And I hope she's not allergic to those flowers I put in there.

PETER: You spent money on *flowers?* For a *vegetarian?*

OLIVE: I want her to feel at home. Alice always says, it's important to be a good hostess.

*A knock at the door. OLIVE runs to the left side of the stage.*

PETER: It's not the fifty yard dash Olive! Keep your hair on.

*JOHN and KATE enter. OLIVE hugs JOHN tightly.*

JOHN: Hi Mom. It's good to see you.

OLIVE: And this must be Kate!

KATE: Yes. It's nice to meet you Mrs. Richards.

OLIVE: *(Hugging KATE.)* Oh Kate, call me Olive! We've heard so much about you!

PETER: You OK son? Your mother hug you to death?

JOHN: *(Laughs.)* Not quite. Good to be home, Dad. *(JOHN takes KATE to PETER.)* Dad, this is Kate Allen.

KATE: Mr. Richards…

OLIVE: Oh call him Peter!

KATE: Peter, it's great to meet you. John talks about you a lot.

PETER: Yeah. Well. Hello.

OLIVE: Now, you two sit down. Kate, tell us about yourself. We're so glad to meet you. I'll get you some coffee. And there's muffins on the table.

KATE: Oh, that'd be great Mrs.… Olive.

PETER: You might want to steer clear of those muffins John. Your mother's put *vegetables* in them.

KATE: Oh! Carrot muffins! *(She takes a bite.)* These are wonderful!

*OLIVE gives PETER an "I told you so" look. JOHN takes a bite, and makes a face. As she talks, OLIVE goes to the kitchen and gets JOHN a cinnamon bun.*

OLIVE: *(Setting the cinnamon bun down in front of JOHN.)* I shouldn't be surprised.

*JOHN butters his cinnamon bun, using the same mannerisms as PETER.*

OLIVE: John—you haven't asked about Denise and Charlie yet. Kate—Denise is John's sister. Her husband Kevin owns the machine dealership in town. They're doing really well.

PETER: Hmmmph. Living in town.

OLIVE: Kevin's taken over the dealerships in two other towns. And their two twin boys, Blaine and Brad, well they're just so cute. Oh, I wish I had a picture of them in their little hockey uniforms to show you. And Denise is just so busy. Still working at the hospital.

PETER: What? Since when does Denise work at the hospital?

OLIVE: Peter, you know that.

JOHN: And Charlie?

PETER: No change there.

OLIVE: Charlie's the youngest. He still has that early morning shift at the radio station your father *pretends* not to like.

KATE: Wow. The morning shift—he must be a great DJ.

JOHN: He's on from midnight to six a.m.

PETER: Damned girly music. I can't believe your mother makes me listen to it. You had a good winter son?

JOHN: Yeah.

OLIVE: *(Smiling at KATE.)* Well I *guess* he did!

PETER: And you're an expert woodworker now?

JOHN: Not quite… I brought a few new tools home. Have to show ya.

PETER: New tools? Thought we sent you to the city to make some money—not take a shopping trip.

JOHN: The boss gave me a deal on some things he was getting rid of in the shop. They were dirt cheap.

PETER: Oh. Then let's go out and take a look.

OLIVE: Peter! They just got here! Let them finish their coffee. *(To KATE.)* Then I'll show you the guest room and you can get settled in for the weekend.

JOHN: Um… Actually Mom, I…we need to talk to you about that.

OLIVE: What's that? Kate, you're not allergic to flowers?

KATE: Oh no. I'm sure the guest room is wonderful.

PETER: Olive, they want to sleep together.

OLIVE: Peter!

JOHN: That's not it… I… We… We're not staying here.

OLIVE: Not staying?

*An uncomfortable pause. PETER gives OLIVE an "I told you so" look.*

OLIVE: You're not going back to Calgary today? It's a six hour drive!

JOHN: No. No. We thought… Kate's staying longer than just the weekend. Uh… she's staying for good. We thought we'd… we're going to stay in Grandma's old house.

OLIVE: The old house! I was going to clean it for you next week. But nobody's set foot in there since you left in the fall. It'll be filthy!

KATE: It's OK. John told me all about it. It'll be an adventure. We'll clean it together.

OLIVE: Oh John.

PETER: *(Muttering.)* Clean it together.

OLIVE: Oh John. A wedding? Here? Peter, we'll have to get to work on the yard! Those trees…

JOHN: Mom, there's not going to be a wedding. Not right away at least.

PETER: *(Looking at OLIVE.)* Nobody said anything about a wedding, Olive.

OLIVE: No wedding?

JOHN: Its not that we're never getting married. We're just, uh, not getting married right now. Kate's not... *We're* not ready.

PETER: Not ready? Jesus son. If people waited until they were *ready*, there'd never be any weddings.

JOHN: Uh, we, well, Kate thought...*we* thought maybe it might be nice for Kate to spend a little time here first. She's never been on a farm.

OLIVE: No wedding?

PETER: Never been on a farm? How's she going to adjust to living out here?

KATE: It'll be OK, Mr. Richards. Peter. When my father worked in Rio, we lived *way* out in the suburbs. I can get along just fine outside of a city.

OLIVE: Oh John.

JOHN: She's going to cook. And garden.

KATE: And John says I can help with the harvest.

JOHN: Yeah, she can maybe do some of the swathing. Remember, we could've used another man last year.

PETER: Some of the swathing? Have you ever even *seen* a swather?

KATE: Well... no...

JOHN: She's a real fast learner, Dad.

PETER: Geez.

KATE: And I'm sure I'm going to love the place. John's

told me so much about Stony Valley, I feel like I've been here for years already.

PETER: *(Aside, quietly.)* So do I.

KATE: We were on the road real early this morning. May I use the washroom?

OLIVE: *(Pointing.)* Of course. Just out that door and to the left.

*KATE exits.*

PETER: Jesus son. What have you done?

JOHN: But Dad…

PETER: You come home from the city with some girl that's never been to a farm before, and you think she'll just do the *swathing*? What's the matter with you? You know the value of a tractor. What are you thinking? And what the *hell* is she *wearing*, anyway?

JOHN: Dad. Can't we give this a chance? I could use your support.

OLIVE: John, we know you need to make a life of your own… But…living together?

PETER: *(Muttering to himself.)* Life of his own. *(To JOHN.)* If we're going to make this farm work, we have to *work* on it.

OLIVE: I know this is what young people are doing in the city these days, but people just don't do this in Stony Valley!

PETER: We can't just drift through life, letting strange girls run seventy-thousand dollar tractors.

JOHN: She's not strange!

OLIVE: I have no idea what we'll tell the Minister. And what'll I tell Alice?

*KATE enters quietly.*

OLIVE: We're going to need some more coffee. John, you come along to the kitchen and help me out.

*JOHN goes, leaving KATE and PETER alone at the table.*

KATE: It's a nice day.

PETER: Nice?

KATE: It's real warm out. And not a cloud in the sky.

PETER: *(Looks away from her and sips his coffee.)* It's bone dry out there. We need rain—not a movie set.

KATE: Oh. Yeah. You're right. It is dusty. Not quite the Kalahari desert, but pretty dusty.

PETER: Hmmmph.

KATE: John said you'd be starting to seed soon. I'm really looking forward to learning to drive the tractor.

PETER: Oh you are?

KATE: I've never driven a tractor before, but I drove a jeep once in California. And I'm a good driver. I'm sure I'll be fine, once I get the hang of it.

PETER: Once you get the hang of it.

KATE: John's very patient. I'm sure he can teach me.

PETER: *(Toward the kitchen.)* Olive—isn't that coffee ready yet? ... Olive? ...I gotta get to work.

*PETER leaves, leaving KATE sitting by herself.*

## Scene 2

*At the farmhouse the next day. KATE comes in carrying a cup of coffee. OLIVE follows behind, carrying coffee, with a flour-covered dish towel thrown over her shoulder. They take seats at the table.*

OLIVE: I think those are going to turn out just fine.

KATE: I do too! I was hoping I'd learn to make pies while I'm here. I've never known anyone that knew how.

OLIVE: *(In disbelief.)* You've never known anyone that could make pie?

KATE: No, I don't think so.

OLIVE: Well isn't that something! Pies are so common out here, it didn't occur to me that everyone didn't make them.

KATE: Maybe I could make a couple more after supper, for that...what was it...U...W...C...lunch you were talking about? It's tomorrow, right?

OLIVE: Oh... Well... That would be awfully nice of you, Kate. But...we... we...don't usually have pie at the United Church Women's luncheons.

KATE: Maybe I could take something else? Sandwiches, maybe? I'm looking forward to meeting some of the women in town.

OLIVE: *(Awkwardly.)* I... I'm...I'm not sure the UCW is taking new members[2].

KATE: Oh. I see... So. I was meaning to ask you. Where did you get that beautiful antique cabinet in the kitchen?

OLIVE: Antique cabinet... Oh. You don't mean Grandma's old sideboard, do you?

KATE: Yes, the sideboard. It's gorgeous!

OLIVE: Are you kidding?

KATE: No! It's so well made. Where did you find it?

OLIVE: Find it? It was in my grandmother's house. I've been trying to convince Peter to get me a new one to replace it. Something more modern.

KATE: Oh, don't do that. It's lovely. Imagine. A family heirloom. We moved around so much. We never could've packed something as heavy as that along with us.

OLIVE: Oh. Oh my…

*Knock at the door. DENISE enters carrying a large bag and wiping dust off her clothes.*

DENISE: Hi Mom. And you must be Kate. I'm Denise.

KATE: *(Enthusiastically.)* It's nice to meet you.

DENISE: It's nice to meet you too. I would've come over last night, but Kevin and I took the boys to the city to hockey camp.

KATE: The city? Which city?

DENISE: Well, Saskatoon, Kate.

OLIVE: Where are the twins Denise?

DENISE: They're outside, running around somewhere.

KATE: *(Looking out the window.)* Oh! Yes, they are cute! Denise…they seem to be standing on top of your van…is that alright?

DENISE: *(Walking to the door and yelling outside.)* Blaine! Brad! Get down off there! If I have to tell your father about this! *(To KATE.)* And Mom told me on the phone this morning that you and John are staying in the old house? How is it? Are there many mice?

KATE: Mice? I didn't *see* any mice. And it's not that bad. A bit dusty maybe.

DENISE: *(To OLIVE.)* Why didn't you let her stay in the guest room?

OLIVE: Well...

KATE: I've had a great afternoon Denise. Your mother's been teaching me how to make pie.

DENISE: Oh—I see. *(She sniffs.)* Rhubarb?

KATE: *(Proudly.)* Yes. For supper. I've read about rhubarb, but I've never actually seen any. I couldn't believe your mom had some frozen.

DENISE: Kevin hates rhubarb. So do the twins.

OLIVE: Don't worry Denise. There's chocolate cake in the freezer.

DENISE: *(To OLIVE.)* Oh. I was wondering what you were going to do with all that rhubarb. Kate, I hear you're a ski instructor. What do you think of the prairies after all that time in the mountains?

KATE: It's great here! I love it. All the open space. I can see forever out here.

DENISE: All I can see these days is dust. It won't seem so romantic once you've been here a while. *(Pulling two framed photos out of her bag and handing them to OLIVE.)* Here's those photos of the boys in their hockey uniforms. I had them framed for you.

KATE: *(Peering over at the photos.)* They're cute.

OLIVE: Thanks Denise. *(OLIVE takes the pictures to the left, offstage.)* I'll put them on the sideboard. *(From the other room.)* They look wonderful here.

DENISE: *(Mischievously.)* She's got room for more photos on that sideboard, Kate...since you're staying and all.

It would be nice for the twins to have some cousins.

KATE: Uh…well…let's not rush things.

OLIVE: Denise. There's something else Kate and John have to do before they have any babies.

DENISE: *(Pretending to be scandalized.)* Mom!

*KATE laughs.*

OLIVE: You know what I meant, Denise!

DENISE: Oh Mom. Just because nobody else in town is shacked up…

OLIVE: Denise! Language!

DENISE: Here's the buns I said I'd bring for supper.

*DENISE opens her bag, and hands a plastic bag of buns to OLIVE.*

KATE: Did you make those?

DENISE: I did. *(To OLIVE.)* You should switch to my recipe. I made a double batch this morning so I'd have extra for the UCW lunch tomorrow.

OLIVE: You might act like you don't care, Denise. But *people* do.

DENISE: Which people?

OLIVE: Well, the Minister for one. And Alice…

DENISE: Oh—Alice.

OLIVE: And just what do you mean by that?

DENISE: Well… Alice is a little…

OLIVE: Well-mannered?

DENISE: Well, yes, but, what I was thinking was that she's a little bit *older*…

OLIVE: Alice is only seven months older than me, Denise. Am I "older"?

DENISE: Oh Mom. She seems much older than that. And all I'm trying to say is that rules are changing.

OLIVE: Not in Stony Valley they aren't.

DENISE: Kate—what do you think?

KATE: I don't know. I didn't really think living together would be such a big deal.

*There is a knock on the door, and CHARLIE enters from the right, empty handed. OLIVE rushes to hug him.*

OLIVE: Charlie! You made it!

CHARLIE: It's two hours on the highway, Mom, not a four-week trip by dogsled... OK, OK. Enough of that. *(He moves away from OLIVE.)* Hi Denise. And you must be Kate. Hello Kate. *(CHARLIE goes across the room to shake KATE's hand.)* Charlie. I suppose they've told you about me.

KATE: Hi Charlie. It's great to meet you. John woke me up in time to catch the end of your radio show this morning. You have a great radio voice.

CHARLIE: *(In a radio voice.)* "This is Charlie R playing the hits". It's nice to hear someone in this house say something good about my job. And what about the music?

KATE: Well, I can imagine... It must be tough to be locked into a corporate format.

CHARLIE: I pick all of the music myself.

KATE: Oh...I see. Well, it's great that you can give the people what they want.

*DENISE goes over to the door and looks out.*

DENISE: Blaine! Brad! Get out of that tree before you fall and break your arm!

CHARLIE: I've always got the latest hits on my show.

KATE: Yeah. That's great! You know...I've got some cassettes you might want to listen to... The Dead Kennedys, The Cure...

CHARLIE: Never heard of them. But I've got Tiffany's new record. I'm going to play it tomorrow. And something new from George Michael.

KATE: Oh. Wonderful.

CHARLIE: My station's pretty popular here, no matter what my family might've told you.

KATE: Oh I'm sure it is.

OLIVE: Now Charlie—you know I always tell people how much potential you have.

CHARLIE: *(To KATE.)* I'm in line to get a big promotion soon. Syndication. A move to a bigger city.

KATE: That's great. Where?

CHARLIE: Vancouver. Winnipeg maybe.

KATE: Wow. When do you go?

CHARLIE: Nothing's definite yet. Soon, though. Mom, when do we eat?

OLIVE: About half an hour.

CHARLIE: What's cooking?

OLIVE: Zucchini casserole.

DENISE: Ah.

CHARLIE: Huh?

OLIVE: Don't worry—I've got some pork chops on the

barbeque for the men. You didn't see your father and John on your way in, did you?

CHARLIE: Yeah— they're out by the shop doing something with a tractor.

DENISE: They're changing the oil in the 46-40.

*JOHN enters, wearing work clothes covered with grease and dust.*

PETER: *(From offstage.)* You kids! Get away from that barbeque! Geez! Denise! Blaine...or...Brad's giving the dog a pork chop. Give me that you damn mutt.

JOHN: Hey Charlie. Good to see you. How've you been all winter?

CHARLIE: Real good. Nice to see you back on the farm.

JOHN: You met Kate?

CHARLIE: Sure have.

*PETER enters.*

PETER: Charlie. See you've dragged yourself away from the record player long enough to come down here for a free supper.

CHARLIE: Hi Dad.

PETER: We could've used some help with that oil filter, but I guess you were driving by too fast to see what we were doing.

CHARLIE: You remember last time I tried to help, Dad.

PETER: Remember? I'm still paying the repair bills. *(Muttering to himself.)* ...Why I let that kid near a quarter-million dollar combine...

OLIVE: You two go wash up. I'm just going to make a quick salad.

*PETER, JOHN, and OLIVE exit.*

CHARLIE: Life on the farm all you thought it'd be?

KATE: *(Smiling.)* Sure. I'm having a great time.

DENISE: Kate and John are staying out in the old farmhouse.

CHARLIE: I thought Mom said something about cleaning up the guest room?

DENISE: Kate's here to stay. For good.

CHARLIE: It's great that you're staying. Mom told me you've travelled all over the world.

KATE: Yes…I've lived in Africa. Europe. South America.

CHARLIE: Why stop here?

DENISE: It's not *that* bad, Charlie. *(Shouting out the door.)* Boys! Get those scissors away from that cat!

CHARLIE: Yeah, right. Not a day goes by when I don't think about how lucky I am to be out of here.

KATE: What? It's great here! So many new things to learn.

CHARLIE: Doesn't take long to learn how to pick rocks and get covered in dust. Give me a stack of records and a studio any day.

DENISE: Just because you and Dad can't get along.

CHARLIE: We get along just fine.

*JOHN enters with a beer. He stands behind KATE.*

JOHN: Who gets along?

CHARLIE: Me and Dad.

JOHN: *(To KATE.)* Sure, for about ten minutes. On holidays.

CHARLIE: Well, we can't all be world class mechanics and master carpenters.

JOHN: What's that?

CHARLIE: It's not easy… Not being a farmer around here.

JOHN: Oh, come on.

DENISE: Charlie's right. God knows Dad doesn't think much of Kevin's business. It wouldn't matter how many dealerships Kevin bought… And I've been working at the hospital for five years and Dad still acts like he doesn't even know about it.

CHARLIE: You should try getting a job at a radio station. See what Dad says then.

*PETER comes in the from the left.*

PETER: I heard that. You know what I say about you, Charlie. I say it to your face. You're old enough to stop playing records all day and get a real job.

DENISE: OK! That's enough. We have a guest. Dad, Kevin and I couldn't make it to the rink meeting this morning. He was busy at the dealership and I had a shift at the hospital.

PETER: You have a job?

DENISE: Come on Dad. What happened at the meeting?

PETER: Bad news. Rink board needs twenty grand for a new refrigeration unit, or there won't be any skating ice next year.

DENISE: What? The old one won't hold out one more year?

JOHN: No. I took a look myself this morning. It's done.

CHARLIE: That's too bad.

DENISE: There's no money in the rink account?

PETER: There's about ten grand in there, so we need to raise ten thousand more, or that's the end of the Stony Valley rink.

DENISE: But what about the boys? They love hockey so much!

PETER: They better start raising money. Maybe they could sell magazines.

DENISE: Ten thousand dollars worth of magazines? That's not even possible. Aren't there any better ideas?

PETER: Not yet. *(Looking to CHARLIE.)* Unless *you* have one?

JOHN: What about the RM?[3]

PETER: I called Roy. They don't have anything to give.

DENISE: This is awful.

KATE: When we lived in Johannesburg

PETER: *(Aside.)* Oh here we go.

KATE: I needed some money to help some neighbourhood kids set up a basketball court. I wrote a letter to the City and they helped out. Maybe I could help you write a letter to the town.

PETER: *(Aside.)* Oh here we go.

PETER: Jesus. There's no money in the *town*. There's only three hundred people in the *town*. Where do you think you are?

KATE: I'm sorry. I just thought that...

PETER: If someone woulda been thinkin' when we put in that second-rate refrigeration unit ten years ago, we wouldn't be where we are now.

CHARLIE: Weren't you on the board then?

PETER: I missed that meeting.

DENISE: This is awful. All the kids are going to be so upset.

KATE: Can't you drive them to another rink?

JOHN: The next closest rink is fifty miles from here.

DENISE: So is anyone doing anything?

PETER: Rob's going to put an article in the paper. He thinks maybe someone else'll have an idea.

JOHN: I'm going to keep looking for a cheaper quote on that price. Doesn't look good though.

KATE: If there's anything I can do to help out...

PETER: We'll let you know. Maybe you can bake something if we have a bake sale.

KATE: Olive showed me how to make pie today.

PETER: Well then, I guess the problem's solved.

## Scene 3

*A few weeks have passed. This scene takes place outside, either on a bare stage, or off to the side of the stage, on the floor. KATE is dressed in gardening clothes. OLIVE approaches carrying a hoe, also wearing gardening clothes.*

*KATE is working and listening to her Walkman. She doesn't hear OLIVE approach.*

OLIVE: Good morning, Kate...Kate? Kate!

*KATE suddenly notices OLIVE. She jumps, and takes her headphones off.*

KATE: Good morning Olive.

OLIVE: Hello Kate. What are you listening to?

KATE: *(Passing over her headphones.)* The Dead Kennedys. Here, try it.

OLIVE: Oh my. *(She tries on the headphones, and appears shocked and confused.)* Oh. Oh, well, I'm not sure this is for me. It certainly is…loud.

KATE: Hmmm…*(She pulls another cassette out of her pocket and swaps it into her Walkman.)* Here, try this one. Jane's Addiction.

OLIVE: *(Listens for a second.)* Well! This isn't too bad. Not too bad at all. Jane's… What did you say?

KATE: Addiction.

OLIVE: Oh. I see. *(Giving the headphones back to KATE.)* So, what are you up to? Does John know you're digging up the lawn?

KATE: Don't worry! Just a small patch! I'm going to make a rock garden.

OLIVE: A rock garden?

KATE: Yeah. I've been planning it all month. We'll have some gravel, a few big rocks, lots of flowers.

OLIVE: Oh—that sounds…interesting.

KATE: I think it will be nice to have a few flowers around.

OLIVE: Oh yes. And rocks.

KATE: When we lived in Holland there were so many beautiful flower gardens. I'm so excited to have a chance to plant one of my own.

OLIVE: Oh. I've always wanted to go to Europe.

KATE: Why don't you go?

OLIVE: Peter would never…

KATE: You could go on your own.

OLIVE: *(Laughing.)* Oh Kate.

KATE: Travelling alone is a great way to meet people. And really get to know a place.

OLIVE: Oh Kate. I'm a farmer's wife! I'd never do anything like that... Anyway, I'm not sure about this rock garden...and all the flowers might take quite a bit of water...

KATE: Well...

OLIVE: And I've never seen anything quite *like* that, around here.

KATE: Well...

OLIVE: Peter's mother used to put a few flower pots out around the house. Maybe you want to try that? I'm sure those pots are in the porch somewhere. That would be easier to water.

KATE: John and I talked about water. We were thinking that once I get the rock garden done, we'll just water the flowers, instead of putting the sprinkler on the rest of the lawn.

OLIVE: What?

KATE: John won't have to haul as much water, and we'll have our own creation—a bright patch of flowers in front of the house.

OLIVE: You're not going to water the rest of the lawn?

KATE: Well...when it's so dry out...

OLIVE: But people driving by can see your lawn from the road! What will they think?

KATE: Maybe the flowers will be so colorful, they won't even notice?

OLIVE: But... What kind of flowers will you plant?

KATE: I was thinking about a rose bush. Some petunias. Geraniums.

OLIVE: Oh. Kate...you can't start those flowers outside, you know...

KATE: I know. I started some seedlings in the porch yesterday, in John's Grandma's pots. And I'll pick up some bedding plants in town in a couple of weeks.

OLIVE: Where did you learn so much about flowers?

KATE: I worked in a greenhouse in London the summer before I started university.

OLIVE: Oh my. Well...Alice always says, 'flowers are the heart of a home.'.

KATE: That's nice! I can't wait to meet Alice.

OLIVE: Anyway, Kate. I was on my way out to the garden to finish planting the potatoes. Have to get them in before the twenty-fourth of May, you know.

KATE: Oh. Can I give you a hand?

OLIVE: That would be nice. I'd like the company.

KATE: Great. *(She pulls a seed packet out of her pocket.)* I brought these with me. From Calgary. I was thinking it would be great if I could grow my favourite vegetables.

OLIVE: *(Examining the package.)* What are these?

KATE: They're butternut squash.

OLIVE: What do you do with these?

KATE: Well, when I was small we lived in Kenya. When my parents went out, the housegirl would bake these for me. I'd eat them mashed, with lots of butter. It was my favourite food.

OLIVE: The housegirl?

KATE: With dad's job, my parents had to go out quite a bit.

Four or five nights a week, at least. Someone had to look after me. So, do you think they'll be room for a few squash in the garden?

OLIVE: We'll make room Kate.

## Scene 4

*In the local bar at the end of June. The table is set with either no tablecloth or an old red terrycloth cover, with empty beer bottles and an ash tray in the middle. KATE and JOHN are sitting drinking beer with a few empty bottles on the table in front of them. KATE is drinking quite a bit and gets progressively drunker through the scene. Country music is playing.*

KATE: John, I can't take this any more. I've got a couple cassettes in my bag. Can you take them up to the bar and see if the bartender'll play them?

JOHN: Come on Kate.

KATE: If I hear George Straight one more time I'll throw up. It was fun for a while. But every day for two and half months?

JOHN: People in the country like country music. Isn't it growing on you?

KATE: Like a fungus. And I don't know how much more of this 40-degree heat I can take.

JOHN: I know. I know.

KATE: Hey, now that seeding's done, maybe we could take a road trip. I've heard it's only a three day drive to the Grand Canyon from here. Or maybe we could head north. How long would it take to get to Yellowknife?

JOHN: Ahhh...I'd like to Kate. But you know we're a little

tight on cash right now. And there's so much summerfallowing[4] to do. And Dad and I have to get the combine ready for harvest.

KATE: I know. The farm comes first. But it'd be great to get out of the dust and heat. See something new. Everything's so dry and brown here.

JOHN: It's not always like this. *(Looking around.)* Hey, look. Sheila and Brian just came in. Let's go over and say hi.

KATE: Aah. I'd rather just stay here.

JOHN: Huh? I don't get it.

KATE: It's just...I don't know. I guess I don't have much in common with most of the people here.

JOHN: What do you mean? People are people.

KATE: I know... It's just that, everyone here's known each other for so long. And they aren't interested in the same things I am.

JOHN: Oh honey. It's just going to take a little time. You're great with people.

KATE: I guess.

JOHN: And didn't you have fun at Sheila's wedding shower last week? Weren't all the girls there nice to you? *(Waving.)* Hey, Sheila!

KATE: *(Grabbing his arm.)* John, stop it. Sheila and I don't have anything in common. All she wants to talk about is weddings. *(In a falsetto.)* "Do you think the centerpieces should be pink or green?" Cripes. Who cares?

JOHN: OK, OK. But Sheila's interested in a lot of things besides weddings. She works in town, she sings in the choir. I've known her since kindergarten. Once you get to know her... She's nice...

KATE: Yeah. I s'pose.

JOHN: Don't worry. There'll be a lot more action around here once harvest comes. Wait and see.

KATE: *(Brightening.)* Yeah. I can help. It'll be fun.

JOHN: Mom will be really happy to have some help with the cooking...

KATE: What? Cooking? I thought I was going to run the swather. Or maybe the combine.[5]

JOHN: Well, I've been thinking about that...running those things is a lot harder than it looks.

KATE: What?

JOHN: Well...

KATE: You've been talking to your dad about this haven't you?

JOHN: Well...

KATE: I should have known! John, you told me I could drive a tractor.

JOHN: Well...alright Kate. Maybe you can do some of the summerfallowing.

KATE: Good. You know, John...you work awfully hard around here.

JOHN: Yeah.

KATE: And you're not making a lot of money.

JOHN: Well...no...

KATE: In fact, I haven't noticed any cheques coming in since I got here.

JOHN: Well...but I'm my own boss!

KATE: Oh?

JOHN: Well, me and Dad work together. He's got a lot of experience.

KATE: Well, that's true. He's been doing the same thing for years.

JOHN: What do you mean by that?

KATE: I've been thinking... A friend of my dad's has a construction business in Toronto. I've never lived in Toronto. With your experience, you could get on with him.

JOHN: Oh Kate...

KATE: It would be fun! Just imagine! We could live downtown. I could get some kind of work. There's a ton of great restaurants. And live music. Wouldn't it be exciting?

JOHN: Ah geez. *(JOHN peels the label off his beer, and is silent for a minute.)* Katie, I love you so much. But...

KATE: But?

JOHN: But I also love this place... What about this? I hoped we could stay here, full time, if there's enough cash. But... If you're not happier by the time harvest is over, we'll think about going somewhere else and getting jobs for a few months in the winter...

KATE: Well...

JOHN: Come on Kate. You said you'd give farm life a shot. At least stick it out until the crop's in. I can't leave before then, and it would kill me if you left me.

KATE: Oh alright. Just...July, August, September... OK. I'll stay here three more months with you.

JOHN: I'll need to be here in October...and remember, we're just going to *think* about it...and if we *did* leave, we'd need to be back in time to get ready for spring seeding.

KATE: Yeah…we'll see. And I'm sure the three…four months will just fly by. Even though your mother thinks we're living in sin. I can barely open my eyes outside with all the dust blowing around, there's no money in the bank. *(She takes the last swig of her beer.)* I'm finished. Can you get me another?

JOHN: Are you sure you want another? I've never seen you drink this much.

KATE: I'm OK, John. At least the beer's cold.

JOHN: Oh alright. I'll get us another.

*JOHN exits to the right. CHARLIE enters from the left, carrying two beer in one hand and a glass in the other. He sets the drinks on the table and takes the chair beside KATE.*

CHARLIE: Hey, Kate. How're you doing today?

KATE: I'm just fine. John already went to get us another beer.

CHARLIE: Can't have too many when it's this hot, can ya?

KATE: I guess not. *(She accepts the beer and starts drinking it.)*

CHARLIE: Hey, thanks for that new cassette you lent me. I love the third song on the second side. *(CHARLIE takes the cassette out of his pocket and passes it to KATE.)*

KATE: Doesn't it have a wild bass line?

CHARLIE: Oh yeah! It's way better than that tape of their early stuff you lent me last week. I wish I could play some of this stuff on the air.

KATE: *(Pulling another cassette from her bag.)* Here! You should borrow this one for a while. You'll love it. The Cure. From last year.

CHARLIE: Great. Thanks! *(Reading from the cassette.)* "Kiss Me, Kiss Me, Kiss Me..."

*JOHN enters from the right, carrying beer.*

JOHN: What are you doing here on a Friday night?

*PETER and ROB enter from the left.*

PETER: Sure is packed in here. Got some room for a couple of old men at your table, boys?

CHARLIE: Sure.

JOHN: Kate, this is Dad's friend, Rob Armstrong.

*KATE reaches out her hand, and ROB takes it enthusiastically.*

KATE: Hi Rob. Nice to meet you.

ROB: Yeah—I heard John brought a girl home from Calgary. Great to meet you Kate!

JOHN: Rob's the town newspaperman. And the mayor.

KATE: You must be busy.

ROB: Sure am! And now that you're out in a place with lots of dangerous machinery, I can sell you some insurance too. *(He passes her a business card.)* Just give me a call. Charlie, good to see you home for another weekend.

CHARLIE: Yep. Let me get you guys a beer. Bud, right?

PETER: Sure.

ROB: Thanks Charlie.

*CHARLIE goes off stage on the left, to the bar.*

KATE: So what kind of paper do you run, Rob?

ROB: The *Stony Valley Review*. Comes out weekly to every mailbox in the area.

KATE: Oh yeah. I've read that.

ROB: So…whattaya think?

KATE: Well, it's pretty good, but I was thinking you might…

ROB: That's good to hear. Another satisfied reader.

PETER: Sure are lots of people in here tonight.

ROB: Yep. Guess everybody's finally got the crop in. Well, everybody but Arlon.

PETER: It's not quite July yet.

JOHN: Somebody's gotta be last.

ROB: He's a good worker when he sobers up. Once he gets going he'll be done in no time.

KATE: *(Getting louder.)* Who's Arlon?

ROB: Charlie, how's that car of yours running? I saw your dad out tuning it up for you when you were home last weekend.

PETER: *(Changing the subject.)* So, John, Rob. Any ideas for the rink? Don't want my grandchildren just sitting in front of the TV all through hockey season.

JOHN: Haven't come up with anything yet. Wish I had.

ROB: I talked to a couple of government guys about getting a grant, but it doesn't look good.

PETER: Hmmmph. Guess we got the last of Devine's money when we fixed up the kitchen[6]. Geez. If somebody doesn't come up with something, I'll be the last chair of the rink board.

ROB: Could be.

KATE: I had an idea Peter. Did you try getting a bank loan?

PETER: *(Ignoring KATE.)* Rob, I was at that new Superstore last time I was in the city.

JOHN: Geez Dad, you'd better not let Sam Stevenson hear you're buying groceries in the city.

PETER: I saw that banker that used to manage the Credit Union. Tom, I think his name was.

ROB: Him? He's the bastard that foreclosed on Dad's farm.

PETER: Anyway, that banker's sure happy he's not out here trying to collect farm loans this year.

ROB: Lots of auction sales in the paper.

KATE: I like auctions. Antiques?

JOHN: Farm auctions, Kate.

PETER: I can't remember a June that's been so hot.

JOHN: I don't know how we're gonna make all the payments.

PETER: Rob doesn't wanta hear about our troubles.

KATE: And it's so dusty! *(She inspects the tablecloth.)* Even the tables in here are coated with dust!

JOHN: Now there's some news for your paper, Rob! "Local Bar Dusty."

ROB: Be more newsworthy if they cleaned this place.

*CHARLIE comes back in from the left with a tray of glasses.*

PETER: *(Looking at his drink.)* What's this?

ROB We don't usually drink the hard stuff!

CHARLIE: I know. I know. They ran out of cold beer, and it's so hot, I thought you'd prob'ly rather have a round of rye and Coke instead.

PETER: Oh. Good call then.

ROB: Thanks a lot, Charlie.

CHARLIE: No problem!

KATE: What? They *ran out* of cold beer?

JOHN: That sometimes happens when it's busy.

KATE: Can't they just send out for some more?

PETER: Send out to where?

JOHN: It's thirty miles to the next bar, Kate, and the cooler in there's smaller than the one in here.

*The men pull the straws out of their drinks and set them on the table. KATE slurps her drink through the straw.*

JOHN: Thanks Charlie. But I'm not sure me and Kate needed any more.

CHARLIE: Oh, I can pay for it. Take 'em, on me. I'm gonna make lot of money one day. *(To ROB.)* I'm getting a promotion soon. Syndication.

ROB: Yup. You let me know, kid. When you get that promotion I'll put your picture on the front page of the paper.

PETER: Hmmmph. Don't hold the presses just yet.

*KATE is beginning to slur her words a bit.*

KATE: I really like Charlie's show.

ROB: Well, whatever you do, don't rush back here. After Dad lost the farm, I thought I'd just stick around a couple of years. Look after mom. Then get to the city. Take a journalism course, maybe. But then the paper came up for sale. And then Collette came to town with that dental nurse job.[7] And look at me now. Thirty years later. Still here in the same damn chair.

PETER: Well, hardly. You've got two little kids. You're the *mayor* for Christ's sake.

ROB: Well, that's true.

PETER: And where else would you go, anyway?

ROB: Shit. I don't know. Guess you never know how things'll turn out.

KATE: Must be pretty interesting, running a paper.

ROB: Well..

KATE: It doesn't get as dusty and brown in the city, does it?

*A woman calls from offstage: "Come on Charlie! Hurry up!"*

PETER: What's all that about?

CHARLIE: Oh, Sheila James is trying to get me to two-step with her. She figures if she can get *me* to dance to county music, it'll work like a rain dance.

JOHN: If I thought that'd work I'd be out there doing the highland fling myself.

PETER: Hell, I'd put on tights and dance *Swan Lake.*

*The country music coincidentally stops playing between songs and the bar is quiet. KATE speaks loudly so everyone in the bar can hear.*

KATE: Well, if the goddamned drought would break, I'd walk naked down the streets of town!

*From offstage: whistles and calls. "I heard that one honey," "Well amen to that."*

CHARLIE: Shit. Maybe I shouldn't have bought her a double!

ROB: You've got yourself quite a gal here, John.

PETER: *(To JOHN.)* Kate's had enough to drink. Maybe it's time you two went home.

JOHN: Yeah. I guess you're right.

*JOHN guides KATE out of the bar. As they leave, there are more catcalls.*

CHARLIE: Good to see you Kate. Hope to see more of you soon, if you know what I mean.

PETER: That's enough Charlie. Christ.

ROB: Calm down. Guess it's time I went home. I told the wife I'd only stay for one.

*ROB exits.*

CHARLIE: Guess I should head over and dance with Sheila, before she starts yelling again. Thanks for fixing up my car last weekend.

PETER: Didn't take long. You staying at the house tonight?

CHARLIE: Yeah...that OK with you?

PETER: It's your room... Charlie, you ever think about coming back to the farm?

CHARLIE: I just said I'm staying tonight.

PETER: No! For good, I mean.

CHARLIE: *(Laughs.)* Paycheques are good, Dad! And I like my job.

PETER: If that gal drags John off the farm with her when she goes, I don't know where I'll be.

CHARLIE: Might have to sell the farm and take a holiday, hey?

PETER: Don't be stupid. I'm not going to *sell* the *farm*. It's been in our family for generations. I'm not gonna be the one to lose it. You'd come home, if it came to that. Wouldn't ya, Charlie?

CHARLIE: *(Laughing.)* Yeah right. I'd be the first one here. I better go—I think they're playing my song.

*CHARLIE exits.*

## Scene 5

*The farmhouse, after the weekend. PETER is sitting alone, drinking coffee and reading the* Western Producer. *There is a knock at the door and JOHN enters from the right with a newspaper.*

JOHN: Hi Dad.

PETER: Hey.

JOHN: Dad... Have you seen this week's paper?

PETER: Just the *Producer*. You have to see this headline: "Feds set up committee to watch the drought."[8] Christ, I think there's enough of us doing that already.

JOHN: Uh... Dad...have you seen this week's *Stony Valley Review?*

PETER: *(Looking up.)* Not yet. Your mother's not home from town with the mail.

JOHN: Oh. Uh... Dad, did Rob tell you about this week's headline?

PETER: Nope. Why d'ya ask?

JOHN: Well...I guess maybe you should take a look.

PETER: *(Chuckling.)* Hard hitting news in the *Review*? What happened? Old Mrs. Albert went to the city to visit the grandchildren? The Smiths off to another polka-fest? Don't tell me Arlon finished seeding?

JOHN: Before you laugh, you'd better take a look Dad.

PETER: OK, OK. Pass it over. *(Reading.)* "Stony Valley woman vows to run naked down main street if drought breaks." Oh Christ.

JOHN: There's more.

PETER: Jesus Christ, you read it. *(PETER thrusts the paper into JOHN's hand.)*

JOHN: *(Sighs.)* "Kate Allen, twenty-five, newcomer to Stony Valley has had enough of the drought. After eight weeks of enduring heat, dust, and grasshoppers at Peter and John Richards' farm, Kate Allen finally hit the breaking point. On Friday June twenty-fourth at the Stony Valley Inn, in front of several witnesses, Miss Allen promised that, if only the drought would break, she would run naked down Main Street."

PETER: Jesus. Jesus Christ.

JOHN: "Miss Allen moved to the Richards farm in April, after she met John Richards in Calgary, where John was working as a woodworker's assistant for the winter to supplement the farm income."

PETER: Supplement the farm income?

JOHN: Dad.

PETER: "Supplement the farm income"? Where the hell does Rob get off. Telling the whole town about my farm income. Geez, that guy's got a lot of nerve. Christ. His family couldn't hang on to their own farm, and now he thinks he can comment on mine? Christ.

*OLIVE enters from the right, carrying a handful of mail in one hand and waving the* Stony Valley Review *in the other.*

OLIVE: Peter, have you seen this!

PETER: Just seeing it now.

OLIVE: Peter, I thought you and that man were friends!

PETER: I thought so too.

OLIVE: Everyone at Stevenson's was talking about us. It was bad enough when they just *thought* John was living in sin. Now they know. And all the men are praying for rain!

PETER: Christ.

OLIVE: Oh, I'll just die if Alice has seen this. Oh, I hope Alice hasn't seen it.

PETER: Alice? You're worried about Alice?

OLIVE: How on earth did this happen?

JOHN: Well, we were in the bar, and they ran out of beer so Charlie started buying doubles, and then everybody kept complaining about the drought…

OLIVE: And Kate said she wanted to run around naked?

JOHN: She was just upset about all the complaining, and the heat. That's all. She didn't *mean* it.

OLIVE: Has Kate seen the paper?

JOHN: Yeah.

OLIVE: And what does she say?

JOHN: Well…

OLIVE: Well?

JOHN: Well, she thinks it's kinda…funny.

PETER: That's just what I'd expect from a city girl. Living out here is not some kind of a game for us. These people are going to be our neighbours until we die.

OLIVE: This is just awful. I never want to go to town again. I have a Farm Women's meeting tonight. I think I'll tell them I'm not feeling well.

JOHN: Maybe it'll blow over. People will forget. Or they'll think it's a joke.

PETER: Maybe that's what we can do…just pretend the whole thing is a joke. Laugh about it when people bring it up. *(He fakes a laugh, pathetically.)* Maybe they'll forget.

OLIVE: Maybe you're right Peter. Everyone's forgotten about Ronnie Waton's boy.

PETER: And that *"friend"* he brought home from Vancouver.

JOHN: And how Rob caught the two of them kissing behind Stevenson's store.

OLIVE: *(Sarcastically.)* Yes. Maybe they'll forget.

*The phone rings and OLIVE goes offstage to answer.*

OLIVE: Hello? …Oh, hello Rob… Yes. Yes, we've seen it… Just a minute. *(Louder.)* Peter, Rob's on the phone for you.

PETER: Tell him to go straight to hell.

OLIVE: Peter's gone outside to the shop[9]… Oh… Well… Ah… Congratulations, I suppose… Ah…yes, I'll let him know. Goodbye, Rob.

*OLIVE hangs up and enters.*

PETER: Well? What'd he have to say for himself? Did he apologize?

OLIVE: Ah…he didn't exactly apologize.

PETER: What? What do you mean he didn't apologize?

OLIVE: Well, he said he had a phone call from the CP this morning.

PETER: CP? The railroad? What are you talking about?

OLIVE: No, not the railroad. The Canadian Press. The company that picks up news stories from around the country and sells them to newspapers.

JOHN: Oh God.

PETER: So?

OLIVE: CP picked up the story about Kate. It might run in newspapers around the country.

PETER: Oh Christ. And he didn't apologize?

OLIVE: Ah…actually Peter, he's quite excited. It's the first time the CP's picked up one of his stories. He says it's a big day for the *Stony Valley Review*.

PETER: This is just unbelievable. Unbelievable.

JOHN: Maybe it'll work out like you said, Dad. Maybe people will forget.

PETER: Christ. If this thing turns up in the city…we'll be the laughingstock of the whole area. Maybe the whole province. My grandfather, my father, me. We've all spent our lives here trying to build respect. Then you bring some city girl out here, and everything we've worked for is lost.

JOHN: Jesus Dad, Kate makes one comment in the bar and our lives are ruined forever? Get your head out of the sand.

PETER: You're the one that needs to get your head out! It's like you didn't grow up here at all. Sometimes I can't believe you're my son.

OLIVE: Peter…

JOHN: I work my ass off for this farm. I work night and day, right beside you. And then as soon as I turn my back for half a second, you're criticizing Kate, and you're off talking to Charlie.

PETER: Charlie? What's he got to do with this?

JOHN: Don't play dumb. I know what went on in the bar after Kate and I left on Friday night.

OLIVE: What's this?

PETER: Nothing, Olive. It's nothing.

JOHN: Oh yeah, Mom. It's nothing alright. It's just that I've worked all my life for this farm and as soon as I start to settle in, Dad's trying to talk Charlie into coming home and taking it away from me.

PETER: John…

JOHN: Don't deny it. Charlie told me you asked him if he'd come back to the farm.

OLIVE: What is going on, Peter?

PETER: I can see it coming. Kate'll drag you off someplace, and I'll be left out here shoveling wheat all by myself.

JOHN: Oh. I see. So you do want Charlie around as a back-up plan?

PETER: I have spent my whole life on this farm. It's too important. I can't take a chance now.

JOHN: Oh…this really takes the cake. I've been working like a maniac all summer. I gave up all kinds of opportunities to come here. And you think you need a back-up plan. I've had about all I can take.

OLIVE: John, don't go yet, I don't think we're done here.

JOHN: We're done here alright. Dad. You're right. You do need a back-up plan.

*JOHN leaves, slamming the door behind him. PETER stomps off to the kitchen, leaving OLIVE alone.*

*End of Act One.*

# Act Two

## Scene 1

*In the garden, immediately after the close of Act One. KATE is wearing gardening clothes. She is looking around, bewildered, holding a handful of mangled flowers. OLIVE enters, frantic.*

OLIVE: Have you seen John?

KATE: Yes! What's going on? He just came storming through here. Trampling all over the geraniums, telling me to pack my bags. He wasn't even making sense.

OLIVE: Which way did he go?

KATE: To the house. What's happening?

OLIVE: Peter and John had a fight.

KATE: They always fight.

OLIVE: Not like this. Things have been said that can't be taken back.

KATE: What?

OLIVE: And now John says he's leaving.

KATE: For the winter. After harvest.

OLIVE: Now. For good.

KATE: Now? What? Peter can't take the crop off without John.

OLIVE: I know.

KATE: And John loves harvest.

OLIVE: I know.

KATE: Well...we were going to go anyway...

OLIVE But not like this... Alright Kate. You find John. Don't let him leave. You try to calm him down and I'll go deal with Peter.

## Scene 2

*The farmhouse. Two days later. PETER is at the table with coffee and a newspaper. There is a plate of muffins on the table.*

PETER: Hmmph. Carrot.

*He looks around furtively, and takes a bite of the muffin.*

That's not as bad as it looks.

*Knock at the door. PETER hides the rest of the muffin under his newspaper.*

Come on in.

*ROB enters, carrying a newspaper.*

You've got a lot of nerve, showing your face around here.

ROB: Peter. We've been friends since we were ten. We're not going to stop now over a lousy article in a two-bit small town newspaper.

PETER: Come on. You know it's turning into more than that. Olive can hardly hold her head up in town. She didn't even go to the last Farm Women's meeting.

ROB: Oh come on Peter. You know this'll blow over. It didn't take long for people to forget all about Ronnie Watson's boy.

PETER: Yeah. Right.

ROB: Oh come on, Peter.

PETER: Ah jeez. Have a seat.

ROB: Got any coffee?

PETER: In the kitchen. Help yourself.

*PETER reads his newspaper while ROB exits to the left and shouts from the kitchen.*

ROB: Is Olive hiding any cinnamon buns or anything in here anywhere? The kids were screaming this morning—I didn't get breakfast.

PETER: Look around for yourself! I can't hardly get her to cook anything lately. And she had *granola* for breakfast. We've eaten eggs together every morning since 1958. I don't know what's got into that woman!

*ROB comes back in and sits by PETER.*

ROB: *(Waving the newspaper he's brought with him.)* Boy there's sure a lot of grasshoppers out there, eh? I just came ten miles from town and my grill's covered already. That burning smell makes me want to puke.

PETER: What's with that paper? Not another article about us?

ROB: No. No. It's just that the *Star Phoenix* ran my story. I thought I'd better bring it out. In case you hadn't seen it.

PETER: *(He grabs the newspaper and looks at the front page.)* Oh Christ. Will it never end? *(Reading aloud.)* "Lady Godiva to Run in Stony Valley." Jesus.

ROB: It's nothing new. It's the same article I ran in the *Stony Valley Review* two days ago. Just a different headline, that's all.

PETER: Jesus.

ROB: After all these years I've been writing, this is the first time my work's been picked up by a city newspaper. *(Pointing.)* Look at that—they gave me a byline.

PETER: *(Sarcastic.)* Well at least somebody's got something good outta this.

ROB: Look. I just put it in as a joke, you know? With the drought, and the dust and the rink and all, I just wanted to give people something to smile about.

PETER: Oh they're smiling.

ROB: I never thought it would go anywhere. I mean, how many people read the *Stony Valley Review* after all?

PETER: Well...yeah. I guess.

*Knock at the door. KATE enters.*

KATE: Hi Peter. Rob.

ROB: You holding up OK?

KATE: Yes. I just came over to talk to Peter.

*KATE takes a seat, and notices the lump in the paper. She picks it up, and sees the muffin with a bite out of it. She looks at PETER and smiles while he glares back.*

ROB: I'm real sorry this's gone so far, Kate.

KATE: It isn't your fault, Rob.

ROB: You heard about the *Star Phoenix?*

*KATE glances down at the paper.*

KATE: Yeah. Charlie was reading it out loud on the radio.

PETER: Christ.

KATE: Hey—they gave you the byline!

ROB: Yeah, they did.

PETER: Byline? The *Star Phoenix* reports that you're gonna run around naked, and all you care about is the byline?

KATE: I'm sure people will understand it's just a joke. They'll know I didn't mean it. *(To PETER.)* Even you have to admit it's pretty funny.

PETER: Oh, it's funny alright. Real funny. Until it rains.

ROB: I think I'll get going. Talk to you later. Bye Kate.

KATE: See you, Rob.

*ROB exits.*

KATE: I see you're trying the muffins.

PETER: Don't start with me. It's bad enough you're influencing my son.

KATE: OK. OK. Look. John told me what happened between you two yesterday.

PETER: Did he send you over here?

KATE: No. I think we both know John doesn't want to leave until after harvest. This farm is really important to him. He's been working hard since he got here. And it's not like Charlie could just quit his job without giving notice, or like Charlie would even come back here anyway. I think we both know you don't want John to go. If you just ask him to stay I'm sure…

PETER: I'm not asking anyone to stay.

KATE: But how are you going to get this crop in on your own?

*JOHN yells from offstage.*

JOHN: Kate? Kate? Are you in there?

KATE: Yes!

*JOHN enters.*

JOHN: What the hell are you doing over here?

KATE: Planning the harvest.

JOHN: It's settled. We're going.

KATE: Oh come on. You'll be miserable if you're anywhere but inside the grain truck this fall. And your dad can't do the job without you.

JOHN: That's for sure.

KATE: John. Sit down. We're not going anywhere. Not before the crop's off. Sit down. I'll get you both some coffee.

*OLIVE and DENISE enter from outside, talking, while KATE is pouring coffee. OLIVE has KATE's Walkman with her—she has been wearing it out in the garden.*

OLIVE: I have no idea why I'm bothering with that garden. Between the drought and the grasshoppers nothing's growing but the potatoes and the squash, and we'll be lucky to have enough of them for a decent meal. Without Kate, I would've given up on the weeding all together. You know...it would be a lot less trouble not to plant a garden at all.

DENISE: *(Horrified.)* Mom! You always plant a garden!

PETER: Don't talk crazy Olive. Where else would we get corn on the cob?

OLIVE: The Hutterites[10] sell perfectly good vegetables. *(OLIVE realizes that KATE and JOHN are in the room.)* John. Kate. What's going on?

PETER: Nothing's going on Olive. This is a farm. We're talking about farming.

OLIVE: Alright. Alright. John, it's nice to see you here.

PETER: Ah. Let the kid drink his coffee in peace, Olive.

DENISE: So you've all seen the *Star Phoenix?*

KATE: We heard about it. I'm so sorry this has gone so far.

OLIVE: It's not your fault, dear.

DENISE: Anyway, I've been thinking about the rink.

PETER: The rink?

DENISE: We need to raise money.

PETER: Yeah.

DENISE: Well, people are tired of fund raisers. Dinners. Raffles. There's already been at least six raffles in town this year.

OLIVE: *(Counting on her fingers.)* Seven, I think…if you count the 4-H quilt.

DENISE: I was thinking, maybe we could sell tickets to an event.

OLIVE: What kind of event?

*DENISE picks up the paper and points at the front page.*

DENISE: Look at this. Stony Valley's getting free publicity. People are interested.

PETER: People don't have enough to do.

DENISE: Tickets. We'll sell tickets.

PETER: What?

JOHN: What in hell are you talking about?

DENISE: If three hundred people each paid thirty dollars to see Kate run down the street we'd almost have enough money to fix the rink.

PETER: Geez Denise.

OLIVE: Denise!

JOHN: Are you out of your mind?

KATE: This might not be the best timing, Denise.

DENISE: Look, I know this seems a little crazy, but think of it this way. If we plan this right, we can keep the rink going, and you'll all look like heroes.

JOHN: Except that Kate and I could never show our faces around here again.

PETER: Hmm.

OLIVE: Denise, I know you're worried about the rink, but this is a bit much.

KATE: Besides, we don't know when it'll rain. Or if it'll rain.

DENISE: We sell tickets, and the first time there's a forecast for more than an eighty per cent chance of rain, we announce it on the radio. The next day, if it rains, Kate runs at—say—two o'clock. They get a show. If it doesn't rain, we refund half their money.

OLIVE: Oh Denise.

JOHN: Oh that's just what we need, Denise. Kate putting on a show for the whole town.

PETER: Some kind of nudie show. Hmmph.

DENISE: If it doesn't rain, we'll have half the ticket money.

And if it rains— we can sell coffee from the rink concession. And baking too.

JOHN: Denise! The next thing ya know you'll be making T-shirts with naked pictures of my girlfriend on them.

DENISE: *(Looking thoughtful.)* Hmmm.

OLIVE: How would you charge people to see Main Street?

DENISE: We could block off the streets, and set up the new bleachers in front of Stevenson's store.

PETER: New bleachers?

DENISE: The old bleachers are falling apart.

OLIVE: That's true. The last time we went to a ball game, Alice got a sliver.

JOHN: We're not selling tickets to see my girlfriend naked!

PETER: This is the stupidest thing I've ever heard

DENISE: Do you have a better idea?... We can sell tickets at Sports Day. Charlie can sell some in the city. In fact, I talked to Charlie already this morning. He thinks the radio station will sponsor us.

PETER: Geez.

DENISE: He's already thinking up a slogan.

JOHN: I can't believe you people! What's the matter with you?

OLIVE: Don't get angry John. Obviously, Kate's not really going to do this.

DENISE: We just need to get the town to give us a permit— to block off the street. We'll advertise it as a "parade," and keep the kids out of the bleachers.

PETER: Oh geez.

DENISE: Rob'll give us a permit as soon as we get the paperwork done.

PETER: Rob's heard about this?

DENISE: He thinks it's a great idea.

PETER: Oh geez.

JOHN: Oh geez.

OLIVE: Alright. That's enough. Kate's not going to do this.

JOHN: Of course not. Right Kate? ...Kate?

KATE: Well...

JOHN: Kate! Don't be ridiculous!

KATE: That T-shirt idea is a bit much, but...the rink is pretty important to everyone around here...

OLIVE: Kate. You don't have to do this.

KATE: Why not?

PETER: Why not? What the Hell do you mean! Why not?

KATE: Why not make sure the kids can play hockey?

JOHN: Kate!

KATE: Think about it John! You can leave town as "the man whose girlfriend saved the rink." You'll be a living legend.

PETER: What the hell's / going on here?

DENISE: It would be different if Kate was planning to stay / for good, Dad.

KATE: But with John and I planning to leave for Australia / right after harvest...

PETER: Oh. / Now it's Australia, is it?

DENISE: We have to do something about / the rink.

JOHN: Kate! You're not going to do this!

DENISE: Charlie's not really coming home to farm?

PETER: He can't work at a radio station forever.

OLIVE: *(After the others stop talking.)* I don't think we've settled this yet.

## Scene 3

*A field. Two weeks later. The stage is empty, or they are on the floor. Tractor noise comes from offstage. JOHN enters, waving his arms frantically to get KATE's attention. The tractor noise stops abruptly, and KATE enters, as if she has just stepped down from the tractor, wearing a dirty denim shirt.*

JOHN: Kate! Kate! Didn't I tell you! Let the tractor cool down before you shut it off?

KATE: Don't be silly! It's not going to cool down. It must be thirty-five degrees out here.

JOHN: Thirty-six.

KATE: See? How do you think it's going to cool down?

JOHN: Well you're supposed to…oh, never mind.

KATE: Anyway, this is a lot of fun! I'm so glad you taught me how! But I'm not quite done this field yet...

JOHN: That's why I'm here.

KATE: And I'm real sorry, but I'm going a little crooked. After you left me out here, the line got a little wavy.

JOHN: I know.

KATE: And I was trying to keep looking at a point in the distance—to go straight, like you told me, but it's hard to see too far ahead with all the dust…

JOHN: *(Trying to break in.)* Yeah…

KATE: And it's really great that people keep going by and waving. But it is hard to keep focused straight ahead when you're waving back.

JOHN: Kate…

KATE: And that guy, Martin, I think, he must have driven by about five times. And he kept slowing down to go by. Isn't he married?

JOHN: Yeah, Kate that's why I'm here.

KATE: What?

JOHN: Kate, you're in the wrong field.

KATE: What do you mean? You brought me out here.

JOHN: Well, I brought you out to the field just north of here…

KATE: Oh…

JOHN: You must've taken a wrong turn a ways back… You've been summerfallowing Martin's durum[11] crop for the last hour or so.

KATE: Oh…

JOHN: Maybe when you were doing all that waving at the cars going by, you might've remembered that we don't *have* any land by this road?

KATE: But…well, John… Oh no. It all looks the same to me!

JOHN: *(Laughing a bit.)* I know. Martin didn't have much of a crop anyhow. I'm not surprised you couldn't recognize it.

KATE: How mad is he?

JOHN: He says you've saved him from harvesting this mess. He offered to pay for our gas.

KATE: Oh John. I'm sorry. I didn't realize this would be so hard! It looked so easy when I saw you and your dad doing it.

JOHN: Don't worry. No real harm done. Hey, Sheila phoned, looking for you. Something about the ticket sales, I think.

KATE: Yeah. Do you know she spent a year living in Finland on some kind of exchange? Why didn't you tell me that?

JOHN: Didn't think of it.

KATE: It's too bad I suppose. I've just started making friends over the last couple of weeks. But in a couple of months, harvest will be done, and we'll be on our way down under. And everyone will've seen me naked.

JOHN: I don't want you to go through with this.

KATE: Denise is counting on me. And all the kids.

JOHN: But what about Mom? She's so embarrassed. I thought you liked her.

KATE: I do like her—so much that I want her grandchildren to have a place to play hockey... Australia's going to be great.

JOHN: I s'pose.

## Scene 4

*The farmhouse, a week later. ROB and DENISE are sitting at the table, counting money and ticket stubs. OLIVE is watching, and delivering coffee from the kitchen periodically to refill cups.*

DENISE: *(Flipping through the ticket stubs.)* Four hundred forty two, four hundred forty three, four hundred forty-four! That's well above the target!

ROB: Don't forget! Charlie sold another sixty in the city! That's five hundred and four! Can you believe it?

*PETER enters from the left. Dusty, and filthy, spitting as he comes in.*

PETER: Goddamn grasshoppers! I damn near swallowed that one.

DENISE: Gross!

PETER: What ya got there?

DENISE: We're counting ticket sales from the sports day.

PETER: Here? Do you have to do that in my house?

ROB: Oh come on Peter. You know all the rink books are here. And you won't believe it—we've sold more than five hundred tickets.

PETER: Geez.

DENISE: They're coming in from all over the place.

ROB: I think it might be some kind of small town record. Maybe we should call the Guinness Book!

*PETER gives him a glare.*

ROB: OK, OK. Have you checked out the new bleachers, Pete?

PETER: No.

DENISE: Kevin and I took a look at them. They're great.

ROB: John did most of the work. He's turned into a damn good carpenter.

PETER: Yeah. Well.

ROB: I'm hoping he'll change his mind about leaving this fall.

PETER: Hmmmph.

ROB: I was talking to a couple other guys down at the rink. We're thinking we could offer John a paying job this winter.

PETER: What's that?

ROB: There's a lot of work to be done, and there'll be a little extra cash left over from this…uh…event. And since Helgi had that stroke last month, we're gonna need somebody else to do the maintenance.

PETER: Ah… I don't think so. Not after everybody within seventy miles has seen his girlfriend naked.

OLIVE: We saw the story on the news last night.

ROB: National TV coverage!

PETER: Oh geez.

OLIVE: Peter almost fell off his chair when that new anchorman said Kate was Peter's daughter-in-law.

PETER: *(Aside.)* That damn kid. Peter Mansbridge'll never last on national TV.

ROB: Yeah… I should tell you…

PETER: Christ. What now.

ROB: Well, the CBC called. They're sending a reporter out from Toronto.

DENISE: Wow! Maybe we'll sell more tickets!

ROB: They said this was the first prairie story in a long time that wasn't depressing.

PETER: Ah geez. Not only do we have everyone in the country knowing how crazy our family is, but we have to have someone from the CBC in town. Damn CBC.

ROB: They told me that since they heard this story, they've been watching the *Stony Valley Review*.

They might pick up some of my pieces for some other stories they're working on. Maybe ask me to write some features. They say I have "an eye for a story."

PETER: Well—this is working out well for *somebody.*

*JOHN enters.*

OLIVE: Hi John.

ROB: How's Kate holding up, John?

JOHN: OK. She was having a hard time getting to know people in town, and now everyone knows her.

PETER: I guess they do.

JOHN: She's been getting invited to all kinds of things.

PETER: Bachelor parties?

OLIVE: If Kate's making some friends, maybe you two won't be in such a hurry to leave.

ROB: I was talking to the guys at the rink about that, John. We might be able to offer you a paying job at the rink this winter.

JOHN: Geez. That's great Rob. But Kate's got her heart set on Australia. And Dad doesn't really need me on the farm anymore.

ROB: What's that?

PETER: Rob—John and I've been fixing up that old Ford. Why don't you come out and take a look? Maybe you'll have some suggestions.

ROB: I usually do. Denise, can you finish up these books without me?

DENISE: Sure. I don't have to be at the hospital for another hour.

PETER: Why are you going to the hospital?

ROB: Come on Peter. John. Let's go.

*ROB, PETER, and JOHN exit. OLIVE and DENISE tidy up the things on the table.*

OLIVE: Denise, I've been meaning to ask you. Do you still have that calendar from the university? That one with the night classes?

DENISE: Night classes? I suppose it's in a closet someplace. Why?

OLIVE: I just thought I'd take a look. I was thinking I might take a class.

DENISE: Take a class? At your age?

OLIVE: Why not?

DENISE: Not planting a garden. Learning to cook all those vegetarian meals. Taking a class. And that crazy "Addiction" cassette you're playing in your car. What's come over you, Mom?

OLIVE: Nothing. Denise, even *older* people can try something new.

*There is an ominous boom of thunder, and OLIVE and DENISE look anxiously toward the window.*

## Scene 5

*Main Street, the day of the run. A "media table" is set up for CHARLIE. All actors in this scene are wearing rain gear. They face the audience during the "run."*

*CHARLIE is organizing his "black box" of equipment. ROB is helping.*

CHARLIE: D'you have the time?

ROB: Geez Charlie. How are you going to be a radio star if you don't even know what time it is? It's about a quarter to two.

CHARLIE: Fifteen more minutes.

*JOHN enters.*

JOHN: Either of you guys seen Dad? The CBC reporter wants to interview him.

ROB: Ha! Peter's gonna love that!

JOHN: *(Looking off stage.)* Oh—never mind. I see she's found him. *(To ROB.)* Sure are a lot of people here.

ROB: Yeah! *(Looking into the stands.)* Hey! Isn't that Ronnie Watson's boy?

JOHN: I think it is.

ROB: And who's that with him?

CHARLIE: OK—I need to go on for the pre-event coverage now… *(Speaking into a microphone.)* Thanks Mike. This is your early morning man Charlie R. —on in the afternoon. I'm reporting from Main Street, Stony Valley, Saskatchewan, where the whole town and lot of visitors are getting ready for the event we've all been waiting for. The Lady Godiva Run. You've heard about it here on this station—Kate Allen promised that if the drought would break, she'd run naked through the streets of this town. Last night, the weatherman predicted that today would be the day, and he was right! So—in just a few minutes, the modern day Lady Godiva will make her celebration run, wearing nothing but her Nikes.

And people have driven here from miles around. There's more than six hundred people in the bleachers! Even Premier Devine is here for the big event. Stay tuned to the hits you love, and you'll hear about it live. Back to you, Mike.

*DENISE and PETER enter.*

CHARLIE: Dad! Can I interview you?

PETER: What? Are you kidding? Show a little sense, would ya?

CHARLIE: You talked to that CBC reporter.

PETER: That was bad enough! Are you crazy?

CHARLIE: Oh alright.

PETER: Goddamn people from Toronto. Goddamn CBC.

*OLIVE and KATE enter on the other side of the stage, in their yellow rain gear. The men give no indication that they can see or hear the women.*

OLIVE: Well… *(Looking at her watch.)* It's ten to. Almost time to go. Are you ready?

KATE: Oh, Olive…

OLIVE: What is it, Kate?

KATE: Well…

OLIVE: Don't worry. I'll be there at the end with a blanket for you.

KATE: It's not that.

OLIVE: Well what is it?

KATE: Olive, I'm having second thoughts.

OLIVE: Oh. Oh my. It's a bit late, isn't it?

KATE: I know. I know.

OLIVE: Besides…I thought you were looking forward to it? A great adventure to tell people about after you leave here.

KATE: Well… I've been having fun.

OLIVE: Oh?

KATE: Helping out with the tickets. Getting to know some people in town...my flowers are beautiful... I caught myself singing along to a George Straight song last week. And...at the concession stand this morning? I had...a...a bite of John's hamburger!

OLIVE: Oh...

KATE: And I sorta liked it... And I know John had a fight with Peter, but even after that, John would rather be here than anywhere else. I don't know if it's fair to drag him away. I didn't understand how important this place is to him until I spent some time here.

OLIVE: Oh.

KATE: I guess I've never really been in a place that felt like..."home."

OLIVE: Oh Katie... This isn't the best time to make a decision this big! Six hundred people are waiting to see you naked.

KATE: I suppose there's no choice.

OLIVE: Well... Denise's boys can find another sport.

KATE: We can't call it off! Everyone is counting on me.

OLIVE: I guess you're right...

*The women leave the stage, and the men take up the action again. CHARLIE is talking into his microphone.*

CHARLIE: Thanks Mike! This is Charlie R. again, back here with you live from Main Street, Stony Valley. It might be raining out here, but it is hot, hot, hot. Any second now, we are going to see Kate Allen... And I mean we are *really* going to see Kate Allen.

The tickets are sold, the bleachers are full, and folks—the drought has broken. It looks like Kate's going to make good on her promise to run naked through the streets!

*(Stage whisper to ROB.)* What time is it?

ROB: *(Stage whisper.)* Two.

CHARLIE: OK folks, It's two o'clock on the dot, and I think I can see some action down at the end of the street.

Yes, yes…I can see her now, down at the end of the street. She's going through with it! Kate's thrown her yellow raincoat off into a heap.

ROB: Alright, Kate!!!

CHARLIE: She's running. And folks, this girl is fast! There's a blur of arms, legs, Nikes and everything else running toward us on Main Street. She is one fast runner! Yes, folks, that's Kate Allen out there. And yes, they call her the streak!! I wish you could see this!

She's getting closer folks. The view is improving! Will you look at that! She's almost here. She's… She's… Holy Christ on the cross! She's my mother!

PETER: Olive! For Christ's sake what are you doing?

JOHN: Mom?

DENISE: Mom! What do you think you're doing?

OLIVE: *(From offstage.)* You wanted a naked lady, you've got a naked lady!!!

ROB: Give 'er snoose, Olive![12]

CHARLIE: Yes folks, you heard me right. The lady that's running naked down the streets of Stony Valley is not Kate Allen. It's *my mother*, Running for all she's worth. Oh no! Oh no! She's slipped in the mud!

JOHN: Mom! Are you OK?

PETER: Olive!! Get up and cover up! For Christ's sake!

ROB: Never say whoa in a mudhole, Olive!

CHARLIE: She's up! She's up! Well, folks, we're looking at my mother, Olive Richards, the Lady Godiva of Stony Valley. She's made it to the end of the street, and she's covering up. Well, the show's over folks, back to Mike, down at the station, playing the hits you love.

ROB: Well. Wasn't that something!

PETER: Jesus.

JOHN: I don't know if I'm relieved, or traumatized.

DENISE: Blaine! Brad! You two aren't supposed to be here! And where did you get that camera?

## Scene 6

*The farmhouse. KATE and OLIVE enter together. KATE is still in her rain gear, and OLIVE is wrapped in a blanket. Limping.*

KATE: You don't think it's a sprain, do you?

OLIVE: No...just a twist. I'm pretty sure. I'm glad you remembered to bring this blanket.

KATE: Of course! I still can't believe you did that for me.

OLIVE: Well...in the long run, it's not as important as your decision.

KATE: But...what are people going to think of you?

OLIVE: Well...maybe they'll forget...

*OLIVE and KATE realize this is unlikely and laugh together.*

*PETER, JOHN, and DENISE enter.*

PETER: So. I guess you're proud of yourself?

DENISE: I can't believe you did this. What am I going to tell the girls at the hospital?

PETER: Well? What do you have to say?

OLIVE: What else could I do?

PETER: What else? What else? What the hell are you talking about?

OLIVE: She's going to stay.

PETER: What?

OLIVE: Kate and John are both going to stay. For good.

JOHN: What?

KATE: If it's OK with you, John.

JOHN: OK? You know I never wanted to leave! Mom! You did this for us?

PETER: What the hell is going on here? I don't remember anyone asking me about this. We'll have to wait and see if it's OK with Charlie. This farm's not big enough to support three families, you know.

OLIVE: Charlie's got a lot of potential. But…maybe not on the farm.

PETER: Hmmmph. Geez Olive. Would you go and put some clothes on? It's almost supper time. You should start getting something out…

OLIVE: I was thinking that…

PETER: I think we've all had enough of *that*.

OLIVE: I was thinking that maybe you could try learning to cook a few things on your own.

PETER: *(Shocked.)* What??

OLIVE: Just for a change. And, I've been looking through Denise's university catalogue. I've signed up for a couple of fall classes.

PETER: What?

DENISE: Mom? You're going through with that?

OLIVE: With me driving to the city more often, you'll have to learn to do some cooking. Might as well start now.

PETER: What are you talking about? What're you gonna take anyway? Some gardening class?

OLIVE: Well, no. I'm going to take psychology.

PETER: What? What's the use of that?

OLIVE: I'd just like to know. That's all.

PETER: And just where are you going to get the money for *psychology* classes?

OLIVE: I thought you'd ask that. Rob's going to hire me two afternoons a week. He wants to spend more time with his writing.

PETER: Why is everyone plotting against me?

OLIVE: Oh Peter. Don't be silly. It's not a plot. Just a few small changes, that's all. You'll be fine.

DENISE: Psychology, Mom?

OLIVE: Yes

DENISE: Is that OK with you?

DENISE: It's not that, Mom...I was just thinking...I might want to come along.

*CHARLIE and ROB enter.*

CHARLIE: Wow, Mom. That was something! And Dad, what were you doing out behind the bleachers? Looked like maybe you were getting into a fight!

PETER: Well… A couple of wise guys thought they should get their money back, since all they saw was an old lady. But I explained to them that that old lady was *my* old lady, and they hauled ass pretty damn quick.

CHARLIE: My boss loved my coverage. I'm going to get a promotion.

OLIVE: That's great.

KATE: Congratulations.

JOHN: When?

CHARLIE: Well nothing's definite yet.

DENISE: Charlie, Dad wants to know how you'd feel if John decided to stay home on the farm after all.

CHARLIE: Huh? What the heck would I care? Anyway, I better get going. I just caught a ride out here with Rob to pick up my car. I have to get down to the station and talk to the boss. See you guys later.

*CHARLIE exits. All say goodbye as he leaves.*

DENISE: So if you're staying out here, Kate…I guess you two will be getting married after all?

JOHN: Well… Uh…

OLIVE: Denise. Leave them alone. They'll get married if they want to. It's none of our business.

DENISE: But what about Alice?

OLIVE: I think Alice will have enough to talk about after today.

KATE: Getting married might not be all bad.

JOHN: Huh?

KATE: We can think about it, anyway. We'd better get home. There's a UCW meeting tonight, so we'll have to have a quick supper.

*KATE and JOHN exit as the others say goodbye. DENISE suddenly jumps up.*

DENISE: The twins!

ROB: Oh no. I'll give you a lift to town and help you track them down. Do you think they still have that camera?

*OLIVE looks at ROB, worried to have heard about the camera. DENISE and ROB exit.*

PETER: You're not serious about me making my own supper, are you?

OLIVE: Why not? It's not that hard. In fact, you can start right now. There's an hour before I have to leave for the UCW meeting.

PETER: Jesus Olive! You're not going to *go*, are you?

OLIVE: Well why not?

PETER: Do you think they'll even let you in?

OLIVE: My friends are my friends.

PETER: What about Alice?

OLIVE: Maybe some of them won't want to talk to me. But maybe some will. I guess I'll find out who I can count on.

PETER: But... You don't even have any baking to take with you.

OLIVE: I know. I'm going empty-handed for a change.

PETER: I don't know what's going on around here. But I don't like it.

OLIVE: Oh come on Peter. You're acting like an old fart. We have plenty of time left. Let's make the most of it.

PETER: What the hell are you talking about?

*OLIVE lowers her blanket suggestively low on her shoulders.*

OLIVE: I've got an hour. Maybe I could give you a re-run of the afternoon show?

PETER: Olive!

*The End.*

# Endnotes

1 *The Western Producer* is a weekly agricultural newspaper. It is widely read across the prairie provinces and has been published since 1932.

2 In rural Saskatchewan, this situation is unheard of. Faced with a declining, aging, busy population, most community organizations are looking for any new members they can drag to the meetings.

3 RM is the common acronym for "Rural Municipality". There are 296 rural municipalities in Saskatchewan, governing all of the area outside cities and towns.

4 Farmers often leave some cropland idle (fallow) during the summer. (Every second summer, in some areas of the province, especially during the drought of the 1980s.) This gives the land a chance to store up rain for the next year. During the summer, farmers "summerfallow" this idle land they use a tractor pulling a cultivator to plough up the field, killing the weeds that are using up scarce moisture.

5 The swather cuts down the crop and lays it out in rows (swaths). The combine picks up the swaths and separates the wheat from the chaff. It is becoming more common for farmers to use a combine that also does the cutting, eliminating the need for a swather, but that was less typical in the 1980s.

6 From 1986 to 1990, Saskatchewan Premier Grant Devine's government offered the "Home Improvement Grant Program." Under this program, Saskatchewan homeowners could receive a subsidy of up to $1,500 to cover home renovation expenses.

7 Saskatchewan introduced "The Saskatchewan Dental Program" in the 1970s. Dental nurses travelled to schools around the province, providing children with free routine dental care during school hours. The Devine government cancelled this program in the 1980s.

8 This is an actual headline from the *Western Producer* in the summer of 1988.

9 A "shop" on a Saskatchewan farm is a shed or building where a farmer keeps his tools, and could be found doing anything from welding to changing the oil in the tractor, to drinking beer with the neighbours.

10 Hutterites live and farm communally—similar to the Amish. They travelled to Canada from Europe to escape religious prosecution. There are several Hutterite colonies in Saskatchewan. Many Hutterite colonies sell garden produce.

11 A type of wheat, mainly used for pasta.

12 Pioneers would put a handful of snoose (chewing tobacco) into a horse's mouth to distract it from a difficult spot ahead. In time, it came to mean "keep on going."